HAL•LEONARD
INSTRUMENTAL
PLAY-ALONG

AUDIO
ACCESS
INCLUDED

PLAYBACK+
Speed • Pitch • Balance • Loop

TRUMPET

CLASSIC POP SONGS

Audio arrangements by Peter Deneff

To access audio visit:
www.halleonard.com/mylibrary

Enter Code
3499-3473-7581-7188

ISBN 978-1-5400-0247-1

7777 W. BLUEMOUND RD. P.O. BOX 13819 MILWAUKEE, WI 53213

Visit Hal Leonard Online at
www.halleonard.com

BRIDGE OVER TROUBLED WATER

TRUMPET

Words and Music by
PAUL SIMON

CANDLE IN THE WIND

TRUMPET

Words and Music by ELTON JOHN
and BERNIE TAUPIN

DUST IN THE WIND

Words and Music by
KERRY LIVGREN

TRUMPET

5

EVERY BREATH YOU TAKE

TRUMPET

Music and Lyrics by
STING

FIRE AND RAIN

TRUMPET

Words and Music by
JAMES TAYLOR

HAVE I TOLD YOU LATELY

TRUMPET

Words and Music by
VAN MORRISON

GOOD VIBRATIONS

TRUMPET

Words and Music by BRIAN WILSON
and MIKE LOVE

Slower

Faster

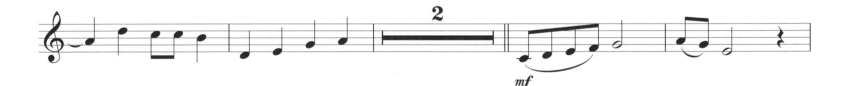

HEAVEN

TRUMPET

Words and Music by BRYAN ADAMS
and JIM VALLANCE

LEAN ON ME

TRUMPET

Words and Music by
BILL WITHERS

15

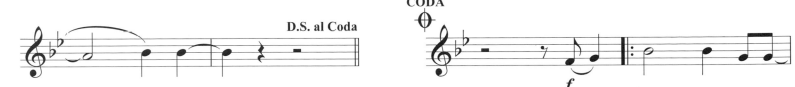

CODA

D.S. al Coda

1.

2.

SHE'S ALWAYS A WOMAN

TRUMPET

Words and Music by
BILLY JOEL

17

WITH A LITTLE HELP FROM MY FRIENDS

TRUMPET

Words and Music by JOHN LENNON
and PAUL McCARTNEY

TEARS IN HEAVEN

TRUMPET

Words and Music by ERIC CLAPTON
and WILL JENNINGS